NO SECOND EDEN

NO SECOND EDEN

POEMS

TURNER CASSITY

SWALLOW PRESS / OHIO UNIVERSITY PRESS

ATHENS

Swallow Press/Ohio University Press, Athens, Ohio 45701
© 2002 by Turner Cassity
Printed in the United States of America
All rights reserved

Swallow Press/Ohio University Press
books are printed on acid-free paper ⊗ ™

10 09 08 07 06 05 04 03 02   5 4 3 2 1

Initial appearances of some of these poems were in the following periodi-
cals: *Poetry:* "The Metrist at the Operetta," "The Dueling Scar," "Manual
vs. White Collar," "Why Geriatrics Are Not Sacrificed," "Watching the
Stopwatch Stopping"; *Georgia Review:* "Stylization and Its Failures"; *The
Formalist:* "Distant Early Warning"; *Chattahoochee Review:* "Oysters and
Other Workers"; *Lullwater Review:* "Neckties"; *Chicago Review:* "Crime and
Punishment"; *Drastic Measures:* "Boxcar Arthur and Other Myth," "Boxcar
Arthur, the Sequel"; *Edge City Review:* "Enola Gay Rights"; *Southwest
Review:* "Venerations"; *The Review* (London): "Victory"; *American Poetry
Monthly:* "Aurora Borealis of the Inner Eye," "Sonar Readings."

Library of Congress Cataloging-in-Publication Data
Cassity, Turner.
  No second Eden : poems / Turner Cassity.
    p. cm.
  ISBN 0-8040-1050-1 (acid-free paper) — ISBN 0-8040-1051-x (pbk. : acid-free paper)
  I. Title.

PS3553.A8 N6 2002
811'.54—dc21

2002066918

IN MEMORY OF

DOROTHY TURNER CASSITY

1903–1999

Self-knowledge speaks ill for people;
it shows they are what they are,
almost on purpose.

—I. Compton-Burnett,
Parents and Children

Contents

NO SECOND EDEN

A Member of the Mystik Krewe

For reasons having partially
To do with Carnival as it
Runs out of steam just off of St.
Charles Avenue in March of nine-
teen forty-six, an Ole Miss end
Has Celestine the Oyster Girl's
Assistant's former girlfriend's breast
Entirely out, and to the mild
Approval of the bar, is, with
A ballpoint pen, inscribing there.
I'm seventeen; I'm underage.
It is the first time I have seen
A ballpoint pen. And now that boob
(The football player) hands to each
And all, as though it were his cast
To autograph, the fragrant globe,
The white geography. I have at hand
The offered whole. What shall I write?
Another writer, not yet I,
Takes hold, and for a moment knows.
The pen is cold; a hot skin tight.
The flesh is there. What shall I write?

The Metrist at the Operetta

By tuning somewhat low the second violins
And somewhat high the first, the two-faced Viennese
Attain the sound of sugar, just as, hurrying
The second beat, they CPR three-quarter time.
Exactitude is not a way to animate,
And, although honesty may be a policy,
It's not a beat to dance to. Face it: in the arts
It is the tricks that *are* the trade. The firm head snap
That holds at bay a ballet dancer's vertigo;
Perspective (false perspective being no more false
Than any); make-up and impersonation; trope.
A metronome confirms clockmakers' art, not this.

Stylization and Its Failures

The vulture, at the least, has not the look
Of flying money, or a Seal of State
Become a Frisbee. Eagles on a coin
Or on a flag, or on a Roman standard,
Look more real than in real life, so strong
Has been convention. Formula and frame
Do not apply at roadkill, which is why
No march from any empire has been called
Under the Double Buzzard. One death's-head
Is quite enough. Upon a currency
It would suggest the god who is not mocked
Is Moloch, and on specie make it clear
All gold is in a sense fool's gold. Not, there,
A logo to encourage free exchange;
Reminder, rather, that we barter life
In kind, to have corruption as return.
Ambitious Scout whose merit badges mass,
Would you continue if you knew the end
Is Court of Honor for a scavenger?
Bald Eagle, Vulture of the Naked Neck,
Are both of you one bird? One carrier
To whose one message there is one reply?
It was mere chance that a Samaritan
Should happen by; mere chance that he was good.
The body by the roadside nonetheless
Would have received attention, in due time.

WTC

Against the best advice,
We put up Babel twice:

Twin towers of such forms
As might be student dorms

For robots—angles right
And tolerances tight;

Barred, perfect as a trap
And for the flame to wrap.

The end in Genesis
Was different in this:

Incomprehension came
To halt the work, not maim.

The last time, possibly,
That language could rely

On making some effect,
If as an anti-act.

Our tongues so long confused
Must fail and be recused

In face of terror. Base
To summit, be its place

The Plain of Shinar, Main
Street, Wall, the Tower vain

If glorious is downed
By envy; goes to ground

With its automatons
Unschooled as to response.

Cities of the Plain and Fancy

Tarred with the brush, and soon to be
Inflicted with the tars themselves,
That is to say, brimstone, Gomorrah
Has the worst of both its worlds.
Too second-city, too remote
To christen, as it were, a vice,
Too metro-area, too close
And too "me too" to miss the fire,
The unpreferred metropolis,
An early Oakland, binds its wounds.
If guests, the Angels of the Lord
Or Lot's leftovers, do not here
Apply for rooms at any inn,
Still, locals have their cakes and ale,
If not enough self-confidence
To say to any watchful host,
"Bring out the men unto us, that . . .
That we may introduce ourselves."
None bargained here for one good man,
Though who can say we could have not
Provided ten, such is the lack
Of opportunity, and lag
In giving up the former Law.
No refugee will be detained
As a saline nostalgia, ties
Of blood not make for incest then.
Such reputation as we have
Is notoriety unearned,
Except as being back-up earns.

No dredge will search Dead Seas for us;
If chance uncovers us at all
It will not change our lesser rank.
Pompeii has the tourist trade,
Not Herculaneum. We speak
To you as Nagasaki might:
Eternally the second choice,
But heart no less on fire for that.

Not to Seize the Moment

A long-advancing change of color, eau de Nil
Overtly overriding green, the tide comes in.
As smooth as contact paper, in bright lack of wind
The East Bay matches glare for glare the Golden Gate,
Their brilliance darkening the islands spaced between.
A former prison one, and one an Ellis West,
They make the Bridge a Bridge of Sighs. Pacific Heights
Has palaces in place. It can be other hand.
So far from Venice and so near the ferry slips,
Art classes—watercolorists—make of the light
Such as they can. It may not come again. Tide does,
Or is not tide. That much can be predicted. Light—
Broad, brief—is prophesied in no ephemeris.
Already, as the sky's kaleidoscope turns round,
And on the dampened paper, calculatedly,
The careful colors run, the even-lighted scene,
So whole, so uniform before, goes various.
The watercolor dries; the turning tide goes out.
To capture is to compromise. Set free the scene
And see its evanescence as an absolute.

Transpositions

Somewhere between the sexes and between the staves
The countertenor makes his thin falsetto waves,

As if the treble clef were warring on the bass,
Androgyny on gender. Music puts a face

Upon castration, as an actor lacking thrust
Might pad a codpiece. Character, but only just.

However, roles in the Baroque were not hard-line
Screen realism, and in art the surest sign

Of desperation is exactly to record:
The nightingale in *Pines of Rome,* the word-for-word

Transcriptions in the '30s novels. Keep in mind
That, once an epoch and its codes are well behind,

Heroic cannot easily be set apart
From mock heroic of the same milieu. So, cart

Before the horse, the operatic stage may see
Cross-dressing and cross-voicing not as travesty

But tribute. And, in any case, it's all a drag.
Castrati had no choice; male altos need not brag.

Orphée, Rinaldo, Xerxes can as well be sung
By mezzos with a good costumer and the lung.

There is a lingering unease in neither/nor.
It's what the certainty fish isn't fowl is for.

Aurora Borealis of the Inner Eye

Not having seen the Northern Lights,
I see them as one sees, eyes closed,
A glare upon the retina.
As spherical as is the sky,
The eyeball pulses to the storms
Erupting from a lodestone sun.
If Eskimos have no more words
For snow than we (and we have drifts,
Crevasses, avalanches, slush . . .)
Have they as many color words
As called for by auroras? Slits
In visors, parka hoods worn low,
Must darken snowscapes which they see.
Rip off the bone, throw back the fur,
And face the zenith. Colors move
There in the windless arctic night
As water, lit by radium,
Would move in slowly tilted ponds,
Or phosphorescence from a gas,
Across the plane of Zodiac,
Progress without a meaning. High,
Impermanent, illusory,
The ions form and form again.
Not gods, not being without change,
Amorphous as the fish, the ram,
Goat, crab are not, these phantoms awe
By presence purely. If you seek
Book illustrations look at clouds.
In silence, as the latitudes

Grow high, and in crisp air its ice
Is crystalline, the flashes raise
Their semaphores whose messages
We cannot know, or bright flags read;
As, when the optic nerve forgets
And in the dark the last shapes fade,
To our own eyelids we are blind.

The Creatures of Prometheus

No caveman was a pyromaniac,
It being much too hard to start a fire.
Obsession cannot wait on lightning strikes.
What could an Eskimo set fire to? Flame
For him is captive on the narrow wick.
It cannot seem the primal energy.
Look to the Northern Lights for that, for might,
As Bedouin to sandstorms. There must be
Sufficient manmade structure to destroy.
You have an oracle that says to you,
Succinctly, "Put your trust in wooden walls."
Who tend the energy it does not tempt.
Stokers are never firebugs. Divers are?
So, one assumes, a few kite fliers are,
No doubt some miners. Water, Earth, and Air
Environ their familiars, breed contempt,
Do not arouse. The alien element
Is that which satisfies. Was not the Moor
Who killed by strangulation—so to say
Conquering Air—in his capacity
As admiral a toiler of the sea?
How many a tiller of the soil digs out
A millpond to his purposes? Torchbearer,
Incendiary of whatever stripe,
Be sure, if impotence is your default,
As theory suggests, a holocaust
Empowers: vengeance as its own affront,
The simple pleasures of destructiveness.

Civilization and its discontents
Are not what brought to flash point your desire,
Except as they put urban housing up
And populate it. Much more probably
It was invention of the sulphur match.

Uses of Hot Air

Which is the archetype of flight?
At the beginning, Wright and Wright,

Or at the end, deep, deep in debt,
The swept-wing supersonic jet?

No birds have wings paired two and two.
Insects, however, often do,

But are the archetypal pest,
In both its senses. At their best

Repulsive, bats have some renown
As image of the upside down.

Unjust that we as skill ignore
Lift-off that led us on before;

If not a pillar cloud by day
Nor fire by night, it in its way

Conduced us toward the promised land
Of leaving land—if yet unmanned,

Flight nonetheless, air lifting air,
Burn after burn the sunless flare

That is revenge of Icarus.
The drift of its rebuke to us

Is, had we kept our eyes on smoke
Ascending rather than the lark

We might have entered safe and soon
Sun's quiet world of the balloon.

Junkerdom in Huntsville

FOR WERNHER VON BRAUN

The models in their small wind tunnels trace
In smoke the vortices of drag,
The voids of lift. And at some lag
The full-scale models take to air and space.

If air resistance is in space no threat,
It is in getting there and back.
Luck's in the angle of attack,
And only gravity's the one sure bet.

A tunnel and its fan are, bluntly, wind,
Not solar wind, and tile heat shields
Ceramic merely. Unknown fields
Might pierce them. Rocket science may have sinned

Not in its dubious alliances
But in its choice of earthbound stuffs:
Those forms of clay it never sloughs,
And tiles are not the earthen entities

I speak of, any more than wind is breath.
As if committing to a plan
To find in Sodom one good man
Or some good thing come out of Nazareth,

Unmanned, yet held to mankind's paradigms,
Robotics probe the universe
For life as we presume it. Worse,
They face a value scale not ours but Time's.

A little overreaching—hubris—here
Might not be out of place. Ignore
Those compromises gone before
(Dividing space from moral atmosphere;

National Socialism brought on tour)
And send, as far as thought can reach,
Thought only, as the only speech
That might communicate with muteness pure.

We shall do well to wait for no response,
That, should its answer ever come,
Would find us long since fossil-dumb.
But, *prosit,* Wernher. Space began with vons.

Distant Early Warning

The sheep indulge the cry of "Wolf!" much longer
    Than the shepherd,
As the danger is for them the stronger.
    Earth is peppered

With the carcasses of those who, bored
    Too easily,
Misjudged the odds. A scruffiness ignored,
    Late, sleazily,

Predation enters. Not until late morning
    Is it costed:
Believer victim; cynic beggared scorning;
    Good faith exhausted.

The Dueling Scar

In being nothing but,
It is the kindest cut:

No spear-thrust to adore;
No leper's shown-off sore.

Upon the student cheek
It thinly does not speak,

Except perhaps to say
A suture is display

Also, and youth an itch
Not for a touch but stitch.

Fraternity and scar
Entirely what you are,

Ex-fencer, is it rash
To tell you that a gash

May well re-open, blood
Wash out its brotherhood?

Back-stab their late *touché,*
Foe, seconds, self betray.

Karl and Julius and Gregory,
or, Are You a Fructidor?

The double afterbirth of revolution,
Land reform and calendar reform,
Hard after dogma, purge, mass execution,
Arrives and tries to make itself the norm.

It doesn't. Peasants' plots cannot compete
With overseas conglomerates; division
Of the year by tens may well defeat
Established biorhythms, bring derision

On would-be emperors and would-be popes.
Had Leninism scored, no doubt October
Now would head our year. Stalin, one hopes,
Was not so forthright or so little sober

As to have given us, to follow August,
Dismember, Sanguinary, Gulag, Gore,
As eighteenth-century Far Left who caucused
Came up with Ventôse, Brumière, Messidor.

Back to plantations: sugar cane and cotton.
Small holdings cannot grow them and survive.
And is Astrology too unforgotten
For Reason's Anti-Zodiacs to thrive?

Sonar Readings

The Soviets' enormous *Typhoon* class submarines are rumored to have a swimming pool for the crew.

—AP

Analogous somehow to lake
Upon an island in a lake,

The underwater pool must act
As bubbles in a level act:

A gauge of trim. And in a dive
(The ship's) what of the crew that dive?

A little relativity
As inner space activity?

Might not their springboard, telltale, graph
Their presence? Trip a seismograph?

Bold swimmer twice immersed, true heir
Of who first left the sea for air,

For your hermetic, late return
Be grateful to the Comintern.

If we have not quite yet One World,
You have, just now, world within world,

Not without end, but still more free,
More mobile, say, than Innisfree.

Now You See It, Now You Don't

No one has ever been invisible.
The concept of invisibility,
Therefore, may tell us something of our minds,
Which can unfailingly distinguish it
From phantom limbs or disembodiment.
The body of the out-of-body state
Is there to be observed. That is the point,
As what was amputated makes its point
By feeling: pain as unseen hologram.
Mirages disappear, but were not there;
Transparent hands of theft that crack the safe
Have fingers, do not work by thought alone.
Anonymous donations well aside,
It is our vices we would have unseen
And not our virtues. Adam hid from God,
Too lately clay to think invisibility
Could fade him out, or knowledge dazzle eyes.
We seem to think invisibility
An instrument—of voyeurism, spying,
Evading capture, finding vampires out.
Not uses that exactly flatter one.
The notion of it may have come about
As a development of camouflage
(Or virtual invisibility).
Mankind the hunter had more need to stalk
Than envy some unseen divine, or voice
Out of the whirlwind, might that does not feed.

Invisibility conflicts the self.
It is as close as consciousness can come
In moving toward pure mind. Brain knows too much,
Or not enough, to let the body go.

A Diamond Is Forever

The stone is set.
Its fire speaks yet

Of molten earth
That gave it birth;

But facets say
Their purest ray

Serene owes not
To clay but cut:

Antwerp and Jews,
Not Transvaal ooze.

Our dearest pledge,
Our hardest edge,

Bright carbon, coal
Exalted, Pole

Star, Morning Star,
Carbuncular

Upon the hand,
Ours to command;

To pawn, to chain;
To scratch a pane

And say in glass
All else will pass.

Oysters and Other Workers

The only jewel that is biological,
Except as greed is biological, a pearl
Is not described in cut or carat. As with flesh,
Its luster, shape, and color, not its kilos, count.
It is its raw inclusion that creates the pearl;
Is it to irritation that the body owes?
Creative as the Serpent's question in the mind
A Serpent's tooth infecting the Edenic clay.
And do the divers whose existence is the nacre,
Like the miners whose is carbon, when the gem
Is in its mounting have their bitterness for Eve
Or for the Mammon who she is at one remove?
The irritant is value-added for the shellfish,
The diamond grace-under-pressure of the coal.
Ghost of the Slaver, Captain of the Dhow, Mine Captain,
Admit what well you know: the VAT begins
At nil; the pearl of great price may have been a black.

Smile Please

I've paid off my debentures
By photographing lynchers.

Above their easy grins
They stare into my lens

As, placing for my view
Their firstborn, parents do.

To keep it sharp, I hope,
I focus on the rope:

A good strong vertical.
The neck twists in the fall.

You want to show the drop
Full length. I never crop.

Lash marks are hard to catch.
I touch them in; I match

Them up from shot to shot;
Touch out the crotch or what,

So I can send by mail.
Nudes have the biggest sale.

It's hard to shoot a burning,
But year by year I'm learning.

Adam with a Garden Hose

Low cacti space the garden that I water,
A little mockery, a fit rebuke.
Before the aloes and the succulents,
The lily's scent, the native spine was here,
A modest desert life-form. Just because
It does not need much water does that mean
It does not like it? Patience has its thirsts.
Swamp and savanna, rock and shoreline go
To make our garden. To have Eden, though,
On each horizon must be sand. The land
Between the rivers saw its limits clear.
Euphrates on the west and to the east
The Tigris. Knowledge and the Tree between.
The reptile of the present garden has,
I see, four legs and not much subtlety,
Except in colors that he changes to,
In panic that is obvious. Hothouse
Or hybrid, grafting and chameleon,
Of so forced consequence there is no fruit.
Temptation ripens elsewhere. Seek it out.
One flesh with Evil, Knowledge too evolves.

Let My People Go, but not without Severance Pay

The Man Who Broke the Bank at Monte Carlo may not have.
He may have been Casino Management's promotion stunt.
The War to End Wars didn't, though it sorted wheat from chaff
As wars go: Reaper quieting all upon the Western Front,

At least until the land mines trip. Catch-phrases, as you see,
Have each a catch. "I have a dream" the Bible counters by
"Behold the Dreamer cometh" and his sale to slavery.
Not only eye for eye, but eye for apple of the eye,

As Jacob's other sons perceived it. On the colored coat
The blood they add will pass for that of Joseph. Blood will tell,
If adequately cued and prompted. Tooth for tooth? Devote
Your life to vengeance and you must defend the jaw as well.

Manual vs. White Collar

The Hofmann Jesus must have made more atheists
Than Hiroshima and the Yale Divinity
Together: limpid stare as through a contact lens
And look of a shampoo commercial. All one wonders
Is, Who was the model, what his later life?
The artist being Swiss, his subject may have been
A woodsman, Alpine guide, or, less improbably,
Head teller at a bank. The cosmetologist
Knew better than to show the hands, lest they suggest
One nailed between embezzlers. Were his miracles
Performed upon exchange rates? Oberammergau
Tenures its actor but conceals his years. One might
In Zurich meet up on the street with Hofmannesque
High middle age: a neatly barbered CEO
At ease completely with the money changers, suave
In fending questions as to his associates,
Himself a parable, but saying nothing Time,
As creeping crucifixion from the inside out,
Could not say through a manumitted Nazarene
Of two-and-fifty. As the Book of Acts makes clear,
Disciples are a form of Board Room, arguments
Concerning seating precedence and all, to say
Nothing of bribery, denial, treachery.
One should not represent divinity made flesh
In such white-collar form as to excuse the mob
That cried, "Free unto us Barrabas" by some hint
There might not be that much to choose. White-collar crime

Sanhedrin and the Roman governor alike
Would be inclined to pardon. Rehabilitation,
Then, not resurrection, would have based our faith.
And what would be its symbol? Fish implies the fishy.

Program Notes for an Orgy

Mercantile people keeping rituals
Of agriculture gods, the Philistines
Present to Baal not gold but golden seed:
Fertility displayed, fertility
Assured. Jehovah, fractious deity
Of rich ex-nomads, earns alone the year's
Whole sins, as gathered on the scapegoat. What,
If sacrifice recaps a former life,
Is offered up before the Golden Calf?
The artifacts of bondage, or the flesh
Itself? A wilderness that never ends,
An aching avarice not yet outlived.
Though at the idol's feet the Law brought down
From Sinai—stone from God's own hand—be tossed,
Such is an anger, not an offering,
Protesting, by its wreck, that in this case
The feet are not of clay. The Calf of Gold
Exacts from us no more than to admit
That we are clay to clay (in desert country,
Dust to dust) and act accordingly.
The Decalogue, its tablets once replaced,
Can be, if nothing else, a useful checklist.

In the Matter of Graven Images

In Afrikaans an idol is an *afgod:* off-god.
How far off? Arm distance, or not even close?
Is he more likely to exhibit female breasts
Than feet of clay? Have possibly a Cyclops eye,
A bauble coveted by White adventurers
And said to heighten potency? Not that a trace
Of that shows on the god's own physiognomy.
Suppose his worship was to stare into that eye,
In whose high color you would see look back at you
The mocking consequence of all you have not done,
Of all you have not seen, all you have not become.
No sacrifice, still less repentance, eye to eye
Means confrontation, is Elijah daring Baal
To strike fire on the altar, bring to life our past
As tall automata might come out from a clock:
Apostles circling on a gothic wall, the hours
Processing in their round charade of open end.
But when we face an off-god it is change we ask,
Not use. Perchance he sleepeth, or is on a journey.
It may be he is the journey. Call him louder.

Sensitivity Training: The Safecracker

Think of it as a handicraft.
> —Paul Armstrong, *Alias Jimmy Valentine*

Sandpapering my fingertips,
By feeling pain I come to grips

With any challenge. If I fail
It means there is no worth in Braille

Or balm in Gilead. Lean near,
Apprentice. Ask if you can hear

Fall into place the tumblers. Doubt,
Or background noise, will rule sound out

In choice of method. Only touch
Can in the end avail you much.

You have to be blind-sensitive
To any tremors locks can give.

Your training therefore will entail
A sort of micro-Richter Scale.

Appropriate. What you would seize,
The gemstones, have their chemistries

From pressures of the Earth. A twist,
A throb, a turning of the wrist,

And as if for the nerve-ends' sake,
Teased out, the combinations break.

Raw, sandings are not fingerprints;
Are selves abrasion re-invents.

Fear only future, Hands-On. Cracker
Then will mean a distant hacker.

J. P. Morgan

Enormous, red, diseased, my nose
Is all of me the great world knows,
Except, I've bought it. If I chose

I could be painted from behind,
And some fool presently would find
How coattails show my strength of mind.

The Steichen photo why retouch?
It does not slander me by much,
Although that dagger in my clutch

Is not. It is the armchair's arm.
All you who view me with alarm,
You are the weak who do the harm.

Markets are chaos, structures banks.
Exchanges panic, break their ranks.
I flog them back. I get no thanks.

Neckties

You Dapper John, you Yuppie-on-the-Spot,
How were you taught to tie a Windsor knot?
"My dad and I confronted, face to face.
I did what he did. Things fell into place.
He tended bar. Weekends he drove a hearse.
We weren't close, but—it could have been much worse."

Half-Windsors are a thing of middle age.
Who taught you how to tie one, Tweedy Sage?
"A mirror. Father stood me by his side
And took me through the motions. Once. I lied
And said I knew. He hated to explain.
We owned the Forest Lawn of Bangor, Maine."

Old Dandy in your four-in-hand of red,
How were you taught to tie it? "On a bed.
My Daddy was the town embalmer. Tried
And tried and couldn't get the damned thing tied
Till I was laid out like a corpse. And now
I knot, nap, twist the ends. A son learns how."

A Different Perspective on *A Rebours*

Accordingly, he resolved to have his turtle's back glazed over with
gold. Once back from the jeweler's, who had taken it to board
at his workshop, the beast blazed like a sun in splendor. At first
Des Esseintes was enchanted with the effect; but he soon came
to the conclusion that this gigantic jewel would not really be
complete and perfect till it was incrusted with precious stones.

—J. K. Huysmans

I

My father, who in snapshots scorns biology
To look like Rudolph Valentino bred with *me,*
I have few recollections of. And here also
It's mock the laws of nature. I am two years old;
He's to his elbows in a paint-store window, in—
Prepare yourself—a living mound of terrapins
Whom he has painted powder blue. The store is his;
The luckless creatures serve as samples or as ads.
A morning in the swamp provides unstintingly,
And brushwork does the rest. Our pastel spectacle
Is stopping traffic, although it is self-defeat,
Since Mississippi in that distant period
Has lots of catching up to do. Art here is life.
Illiterates, on whom the lettering is lost,
Assume the coloring to be an act of God.
But then, illiterates do not redecorate.
In 1933, no one redecorates.
The business goes broke, thank God, or I might be
Today the most sought after decorator there.
I cannot tell you what befell the terrapins,
Nor do I wish to know. A shell of powder blue
Cannot have been a help if Father let them loose:

Reintroduction to the wild as color chart.
I do not even think the paint was very good.
I seem to see it rubbing off on sheikhdom's shirt;
For these, as any self-respecting hardshell would
So tarted-out in painted color, huddle up
And must be redistributed. The Horsemen Four
Take on my handsome father, but you see from whom
I have my functioning imagination. Nice
To say I thought of him and of that color guard
When I encountered *A Rebours,* but I did not.
I did, though, finding on menus in Baltimore
Terrapin Maryland. Does it taste much of paint?

And Mississippi? It is there in blood and sand.
Or would be if its swamps had sand instead of mud.

II

In recollection number two
The swamp is all around us. Des
Esseintes the father and the son
Are on a fishing afternoon.
The elder, who can bring a knife
Edge crease to khaki, does. No one
Could possibly resemble less
A bodyguard of Huey Long.
The younger is an unstarched mess,
But being somewhat under three
Is looked at mostly from above.

Not by request, but nonetheless
Specifically to let me see,
My father from his tin bait bucket
Lifts instructively the lid.
Below me, in a shining dark,
I see the circling minnows crowd,
And even in a summer swamp
I smell at once the primal smell.
It is another world, and has,
I think, not much to do with me,
Although I am not squeamish. Hook

Inside the lip, a bait that bleeds,
Do not disturb me, as I know
Much else can happen. On our last
Excursion Father caught a hook
In his own lip. It took morphine,
The surgeon's knife, and two stiff shots

For tetanus to get him through.
It has occurred in later years
He may have thought his fine white scar
Well worth it. I, though, at the smell
Of minnows, welcome back the lid.

Favorites

I

As if the emperor had had him cloned,
A statuary plague, an ad hoc god,
Antinous infests the Roman world:
One man's obsession forced upon the arts,
A state-imposed and sacrosanct ideal,
Lifelike to possibly the same degree
As was the corpse recovered from the Nile.
Given the realism shown elsewhere
In portrait busts, including Hadrian
Himself, is it too much to intimate
That had the sculptors had the entity
Alive in front of them the face we have
Would be quite other? Did the emperor
Remember, seeing the seraphic clones,
The strapping adolescent of the streets,
Or, having never really seen him, lose
In marble what he lost in flesh and blood?
The chisel creates what the Crown commands,
Enough generic so that, envying,
Successors will not hammer off the head.
No lover sees beyond what he projects.
It is the rival who can see the blank.

II

If Catherine had seen behind the villages
To which Potemkin gave false fronts, would she have seen
Through him? Or is infatuation blind to depth?
And, Russia being Russia, how can we be sure
Potemkin's constructs were not less unlivable
Than peasants' were? The fabled tree that falls unheard
And ceases to exist, when Louis turned his back
Was demonstrated in the fountains at Versailles.
No doubt the empress knew full well when not to look;
And possibly Potemkin, lacking one eye, built
As best he could, not benefiting by 3-D,
His happy lack in contemplating Catherine.

Crime and Punishment

A reporter interviewing Leopold in Puerto Rico after his
release was somewhat jolted when he realized there was
a portrait photograph of Richard Loeb in the living room.

—Hal Higdon, *The Crime of the Century*

"A love like ours what common herd can probe?"
Said Nathan Leopold to Richard Loeb.

"To prove it we'll do something brave and bold,
As Nietzsche might," said Loeb to Leopold.

"A random murder," Nate now says to Dick.
The Übermenschlichkeit is getting thick.

Thus was arrived at, route circuitous,
A Russian novel's "Act Gratuitous."

The victim was a certain Bobby Franks.
No relative of Holland's Anna, thanks,

One being plural, the other not.
But notorieties incline to blot.

Infatuation? Hell's obverse of hate.
Gehenna in a raccoon coat tempts Nate.

The crime poor Bobby was the victim of
Is in a sense upon Raskalnikov,

In that the inexperienced who read
Believe the less well-read do not quite bleed.

Dick died in prison, of a lover's knife.
Then Nate got out. Parole boards know not life.

And at the end, a—maybe—other self,
Freed, Nate has Richard's photo on a shelf.

But why should not he, having killed for whom,
Have for gratuity Hell in his room?

Boxcar Arthur and Other Myth

Nothing has been more literal
Than endings of the Symbolists:
Verlaine's long litigation, debt,
Cirrhosis, pot shots, hemorrhoids;
The ants and bees of Maeterlinck;
Ear-trumpet of the deaf Corbière;
And Rimbaud? Trafficking in slaves,
Or I am Sindbad at full sail.
In Paris rain may fall in heart
And fall in town, but on the red,
Salt coast of Ethiopia
It does not rain at all. A roof
Of tin, a half-height wall of palm fronds . . .
He who is his mother's child
Outdoes her in the wares he trades,
The rents he lives on. In this case,
Yes, Mother was to blame. The worst
Of the provincial bourgeoisie.
And of the live-in hellion,
The targeted boy genius
(More bluntly, call-boy genius)
Much must endure. One would not care
To be a houseboy in Harar,
Or owe the Agency. Attacked
In boxcars by the Army? Him?
As likely as the fantasy
He ceased to write. Who knows, by now,
How much he shredded? Did he use
For pseudonym Pierre Loti?

Their talents are not unalike.
He planned to marry. Whom? *La Veuve*
Verlaine, if he could outlive Paul?
A burned-out Brahms and Bourbon Clara,
Nothing learned and naught forgot.
But Symbolists as a profession
Scorn to be consecutive.
So we, confronted with the tough,
Ill slaver going home to die,
May honor. Only disconnect,
As E. M. Forster should have said.
All honor, as they should, all those
Who have no choice, and bite the shot.
What is the opposite of pack
And follow? Pack, and burn the bridge
Behind one? There are fires and fires.
Ex-trick has cancer in his knee.
If he outlived, like Bernhardt, loss
Of leg and lived another fifteen years,
Would he outwrite that other, prose
Discontinuity J. Conrad
Korzeniowski? Possibly.
Out of the vacant eyes of death
The all-forgiving symbol stares.

Boxcar Arthur, the Sequel

A noir, E blanc, I rouge, U vert, O bleu: voyelles.

At almost two, the little girl
Is notably unchubby. Jaw
Suggests and stubbornness confirms
Grandmother will emerge in her.
Having one leg and no one job,
Her father is enough at home
To see the symptoms. Irony
Of ironies, he finds that these
Attract him to the child. His wife
Has nothing that could replicate,
Except a dowry, which, at eight
Percent, is replicating fast:
Suez Canal shares. He at one point,
Earlier in middle age,
Had thought of trying Panama.
He is an engineer of sorts,
And put by Abyssinia,
Could Darien have been much worse?
It is a comment on his youth
That, leathery and sallow, bald,
On crutches, he at last had true
Success as object of desire.
Whether for dangers he had passed
Or outright pity he is too
Incurious to ask. The truth
Is, neither. Mlle. Suez
Had fantasies of doing good
On Devil's Island, and in him

Saw her Guiana close to home.
Specialized tastes are what they are;
It is not lost on him that best
Of all, perhaps, in terms of income,
Would have been to be a blond
Young amputee of seventeen.
If in a sense he was that—cut
Off certainly from common sense—
The Sazerac that was his mind
In those days now is clear enough
To know it is not memory.
Absinthe took care of that. Meanwhile,
His daughter's mind he is obsessed
With forcing prematurely. Toys
Must teach the alphabet. "At two?"
His wife rebukes him. "Let the child
Have rattles. She can't even talk."
Perhaps. She knows, however, who
Her friends are, and ascends his leg.
The one that takes up at the knee.
Specialized tastes are not confined
To the Parisian underworld.
Her father reaches from his chair
And takes up off the floor, spit out
In the direction of *Maman,*
Her pacifier and her blocks,
That on opposite faces, chewed,
Have traces of an upper case
And lower. Starting off by rote,
"A, black," he tells her; "E . . ." As if
Absinthe gave way to Pernod, vague,
He halts. His version does not match
The color coding of the blocks.

"U, red," he tries again, and brings
In line with late reality
His vowels, as he brought himself.
True blue, the stubborn eyes go shut.
Pernod and absinthe mix again;
His mind drifts to her infancy:
Disorienting days of sleep
Well lost; the hard technique he learned
To walk her on a single crutch.
"Really to totally derange
The senses," he at some remove
Self-quotes, "it takes an infant." Tired,
He puts the vowel blocks in color
Order, shifts his child, and sleeps.

Enola Gay Rights

Arm missing, torso headless on a beach,
The wreck of Liberty, as realized
In movies of atomic holocaust,
Implies that the producers do not know
How bold a skeleton the Statue has.
It might be an immense ceramic doll,
An Abu Simbel part Lord Elgin stole,
Or plastic Crazy Horse not yet complete.
Unyielding inner steel is not, one fears,
A backbone Hollywood knows much about.
Meanwhile, in real time and in good repair,
The Statue says, depending on your view,
Preparedness or disarmament. A torch
Incites to riot or is beacon, dims
Or not as it is fueled, casts a light
Upon the tablets which the goddess holds,
To which, however, no one pays much heed.
As wreckage on a science fiction strand
A truer warning would be Rhodes in bits:
Apollo come apart colossally;
The Muses in a story conference;
Special effects gone wrong, earthquake and bomb.

The Second-Guesser

As archetypal as the Wandering Jew,
I do not wander, mine a point of view

Innately fixed upon the recent past
And by that time's own views not overcast.

I say for Merrill Lynch, "You should have bought,"
And once you buy, "Ought you to sell? You ought."

I always know what doctors should have done,
How any game, or war, could have been won.

As soon as Caesar crossed the Rubicon
I was on hand to say, "Why not the Rhône?"

And when the Red Sea parted said, "Suppose
Before we reach the Sinai it should close?"

Of course, I favored Pharaoh, being spy.
Nay, double agent. Always covered, I.

The courts, I hint, are always hit-or-miss.
He was unjustly sentenced, Alger Hiss.

As Pilate, washing from my hands the guilt,
I'm quick to say, "The scales of justice tilt."

I was for Haig the press that urged, "Hold back,"
That in the Missile Crisis cried, "Attack!"

My finest moment is the après-Bomb
(I was not draft age), or perhaps Viet Nam.

If Little Boy had landed on Pol Pot
Cambodia might be what it is not,

Fat Man have turned the tide at Dien Bien Phu.
Québec is guilty of apartheid too.

A sort of retro-oracle, I drone
My might have been. An armchair is my throne,

Tenure my Camelot. On it accrue
All envies of the do-not for the do.

Estate Planning

How easily we outwit nature. Progeny
Whose number puts in doubt the matter of to whom
Our Earth belongs we sort by primogeniture.
It paupers necessarily the later born,
But, after generations, subdividing does.
Incest is somewhat frowned upon, but concentrates
Inheritance. There is a plotting Ptolemy
Latent in all of us. And those who hoard the blood
And think thereby to hoard the gold will find themselves
In thrall to lawyers, DNA tests, trusts, entailments.
Founding Father, ought the line to end with you?
A fortune is defined as what accumulates,
Which means a prodigal is he who dissipates.
But note: the prodigal was not the elder son,
Nor was it he who ordered killed the fatted calf.
One's firstborn too is privileged to envy, sulk.
Like features, talent, or disease, extravagance
May skip a generation. Sibling rivalry
Is simply father-son conflict at one remove.
The seven good years segue into seven lean,
And unto Pharaoh goes the cry "Release us grain!"
Defying nature's cycles that would have us starve,
We learn to store, to breed a green revolt, to ditch,
Pipe, irrigate. It's only one more step to clone.

I Dreamed Last Night I Went Again to Manderley

Well, no; Johannesburg. I saw again
The gutted Rand, the flattened pyramids
Of cyanide-denuded sand, the plume
On windy days incessant off the summits;
Saw the houses of the Randlords, backs
To Mammon, facing toward Pretoria;
And on the god's own turf, the mine compounds,
Arenas and the dances. Rubber boots
On Zulus in their lethal if unmeant
Rebuke for ethnomusicologists:
A Brechtian, satiric slapping dance
That hints of Löwenbräu and Lederhosen,
Not of assegais and kaffir beer.
The tribal rite is tourists filing in
To fill the low stone risers seat by seat.
And though a thunder heard is too compact
To echo in the drums, the lightning shafts
Add bright diagonals to high-rise flats.
Drawn up beyond, unseen except for breaks
In the horizon, townships stud the veld
Like pieces in a board game, as indeed
They are, Reef land use being what it is.
Beyond their low monotony thin out
To nothingness the tin roofs and the smoke;
And at the end the golden veld itself:
Made real, the very curvature of Earth—
The planet that we keep, or cede, or dream.

Victory

To deal with illness not my own
I'm back in my hometown.
Full circle, in a sense, if not
How closure measures that.

The missing seasons still come round,
The out of reach at hand.
I am not sorry that I left,
For all a self-shed graft

Cannot, I now begin to see,
Fall too far from the tree.
That former life goes on, full tilt.
I join it by default.

Has one whose past and present meet
Some Pyrrhic of defeat?
I'll leave at length; I'll not be back.
I'm far beyond the tic

Of proving something. Is there least,
Remotest interest
In this forever posed "What if . . ."
Except it's been my life?

In the Receiving Line

"Late, too late, ye cannot enter now."
The stark injunction, cold but somehow kind,
Counts off the lamps, conserves the oil, and—Mao
No doubt would disapprove—forms in the mind

Elites of the rejected. I have been
In many weddings. All the fun, without
Exception, was for single Best of Men
And Maids of Honor from divorce court. Stout,

Yet eager to sing any diet's praise,
They proffer cake, drink, straighten Ascot ties.
"Do ring me up sometime." Yes. Nothing says
Some Foolish Virgin may not end up wise.

Venerations

Amusing, or appalling, that at my age love
Should seem a flawed, self-serving local miracle
Referred to some sophisticated Cardinal.
How not to certify, yet not deny outright?
The Virgin on a motorcycle, Christ in corn
As flip side of a burnt tortilla . . . none of these
Is less improbable than Eros late encountered,
Who, however much a scorch, will leave no trace,
A hoax among the others.
                       Are there witnesses?
Conversions? Cures? I am the Devil's Advocate.
I must point out that love, if it converts, converts
The pre-converted, and is held incurable.
A brief, small mystery, to be meanwhile a cult,
Unthreatening, non-binding. Elvis seen on toast.
Beatify. The canonizing keep on hold.

Hanging On

"End of my rope" too much implies
    That "rope"
Was helpful, or disguise
    For hope.

Admit it is the grip that ends:
    Fatigue
Opening wide the hands
    In league

With age and self-deception. Hemp
    Has clout,
But when the smoking-lamp
    Goes out

Is not lifeline. It lets us crash.
    So, test
Of fiber, length of ash,
    Are best

Regarded as the protocol
    Of which
Fate of the three says "All."
    As such

The jealous trio saving thread
    At cost
Of us who hang—chute, net,
    Long lost.

Why Geriatrics Are Not Sacrificed

It is a young man's heart the knife of stone
Puts in the Aztec's hand; heart he will raise,
Still beating, toward the god who, like the priest,
Is blood-besmeared already, as a god
Both death and fear. His priesthood's fear is, flint
Upon an old man's heart is stone on stone;
Might strike a spark that would ignite the world
If there were breath enough to stir the lint,
So much a fossil fuel envy is.
Young hearts an altar never lacks. Its lure's
The name of Chosen: ease and sex and glut,
Our tempting pyramid. If at the top
A dagger waits, hearts calcify below,
One beat, one granule at a time toward age,
Until a sacrifice seems self-reflexive:
Hardened sternum and the stony twist,
Intransigence upon intransigence.

Watching the Stopwatch Stopping

The great fear of the Maya was that Time would stop.

—Robert Kaplan

And if it should? The seasons calmly would continue,
But be no longer measure. Keeping to its venue,
High tide reverse and go unnoticed, no erosion
Confirm the aging of its beaches; drying, Ocean
Become no saltier; rain born of it not freshen;
The rising of the blood not ever reach to passion;
Our racing solar year fall back to match the lunar;
Eternal present merge the later and the sooner.
Radioactive or our own, decay not threaten;
The lower reaches of a water clock not wetten.
Section a tree to count its rings and you will see there
A disc as featureless as porcelain might be there.
Become a tabulated list of random numbers,
A calendar is not some duty that encumbers,
Though Julian, Gregorian, if we endow them,
Exact from us as much of Time as we allow them.
The Maya need not worry; of such bits and pieces
As we spare—and Creation—Time before it ceases
Will bear its sons away. Hearts old and fortunes wilting,
The sandglass turns. It is Time's stream, its threat of silting.

The Ultimate National Monument

Before it had the name it had such forms
Of life as still it has, and faultless stars
Recurring true between the lightning storms.
We call them signs, add meanings. Glaring Mars

And milder wanderers among them drift,
At times the houses of Astrology,
Our pledge of futures, Zoroaster's gift.
Now, magnitudes set arbitrarily

And creatures of a night no more than night,
They shine within their limits. All the same
My own sign, Capricorn, leaps doubly bright
Above the valley of the dreaded name.

The Grateful Minimalist

Aghast
A past

Condign
As mine

Could, bit
By bit,

Escape,
I trap

Its time
In rhyme:

The hits,
The pits;

Some one
On one

Contacts;
My acts

Of spite
I quite

Regret
(And yet

Would score
Once more).

Few works;
Some quirks.

No blanks,
Just thanks.